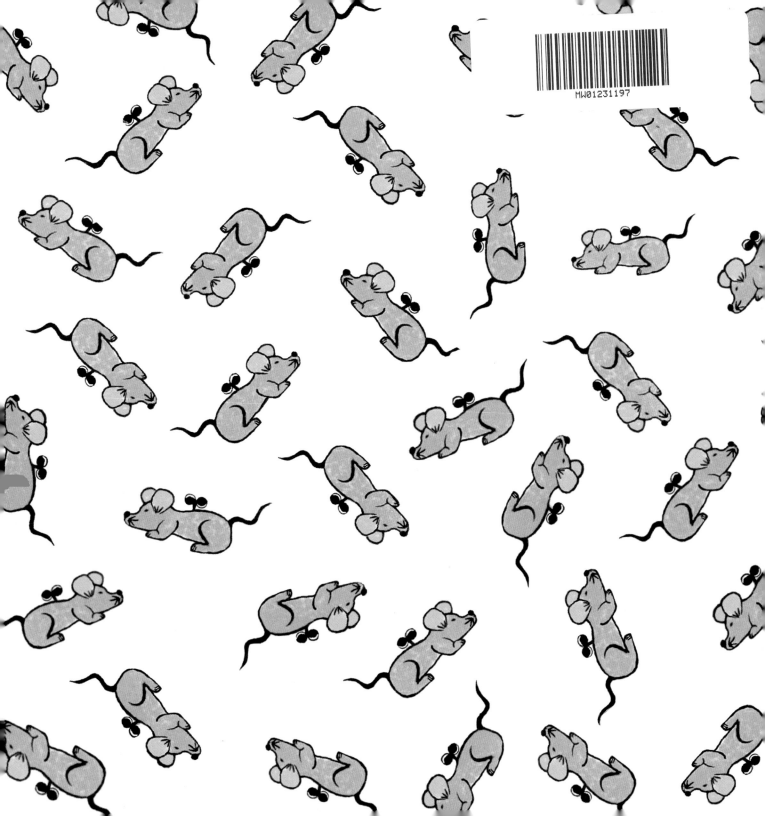

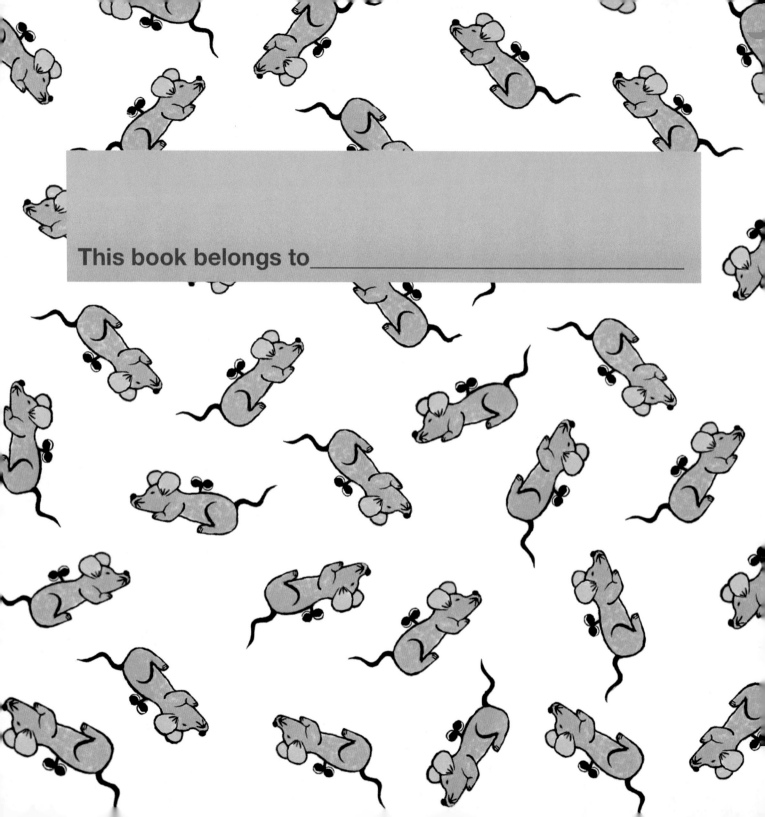

This book belongs to_____

This book is dedicated to my youngest grandson, Gage! He has a smile and a laugh that warms your heart and he has all the kitties. And also, to my brand-new granddaughter, tiny Brynn. She is so beautiful!

A sincere thank you to my editors Peter Huffman and my son Jess Lorentzen. This book would not be possible without you!

Wilber's Furry Surprise!

(Wilber Learns Responsibility)

Written and Illustrated

By

Collette Dahl Lorentzen

It was afternoon on a lazy summer day. Wilber was home sleeping on his big, green, fluffy pillow. Outside, the birds were singing happily in the warm gentle breeze.

All of a sudden, for no particular reason, Wilber woke up. "I need to find Oliver," he thought. He looked all over, sniffing as he went but he couldn't find Oliver anywhere.

He decided to look out of the window by the front door. But, no Oliver. Then he went to the back door to look, but still no little boy. Wilber was anxious for Oliver to come home. "But where did he go?" he puzzled.

A short time later, Wilber heard the front door open. He ran to see if it was Oliver. Wilber barked excitedly. He was so happy to see his little boy! But, at that very moment, he noticed that Oliver was holding something small and furry. He could see that it was orange and black and white. "I have a furry surprise," said Oliver excitedly.

Oliver kneeled down so that Wilber could see what he was holding. "This is a kitten, Wilber," Oliver said. "She is calico colored. Isn't she cute? Now you have a new friend to play with." This made Wilber happy, and a little nervous. He had never had a kitten before and he wasn't sure what to do, or how to take care of her. He hoped that Oliver would show him.

He wanted to be the best at caring for his new friend. "Everyone needs love, caring and kindness," he thought. "That's what Oliver taught me."

Oliver DID show Wilber what to do and how to care for his new friend. "We have to give her food. She is young and very small. She needs the kind of food baby kitties eat. Here is her new food bowl," Oliver said, as he sat the bowl down.

Will you help me make sure we keep her bowl full of food, Wilber? That way she will grow up to be a healthy, happy cat," Oliver explained.

"This is her other bowl, for water. We need to keep it clean so she has fresh water to drink any time she needs it," said Oliver.

Now she needs a litter pan with kitty litter in it. She can use it to go potty," Oliver said. "I'll put it over here, out of the way. And don't forget, Wilber, since we both decided that we wanted a new friend we have to do all these things for her every day!

"That is being <u>responsible</u> and we all have things to be responsible for. We are her new parents now and she depends on us to care for her," Oliver explained.

"Here is a brush for her, Wilber. We have to brush her every day since her fur is so long. That will keep her fur nice and shiny," Oliver said with a smile.

"Oh Wilber!" Oliver said excitedly. "We forgot the last most important thing to do! We need to give her a name. Hmmm. What's a good name for our new friend, Wilber?"

"Rrruuuttthhh," Wilber barked to Oliver. "That's a great name Wilber," Oliver shouted excitedly. "We will call her Ruth!"

As the days went by, Oliver and Wilber shared the chores when they cared for Ruth. Wilber decided that this was going to be great fun and he truly loved having a friend to care for.

Wilber didn't know how to brush her, so he left that up to Oliver. But, Wilber did lick her face and clean Ruth up after she ate her food and drank her water.

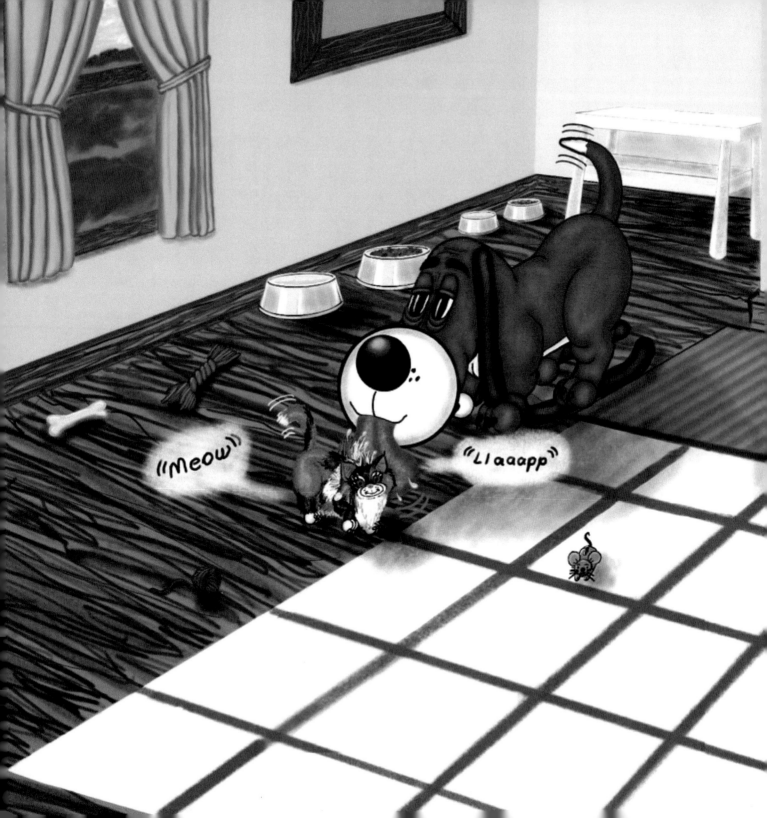

Wilber made sure that Ruth was safe and stayed out of trouble, and stayed out of his food bowl too!

A few days later, Wilber was playing with Ruth and watching over her. The two friends had played hard all day.

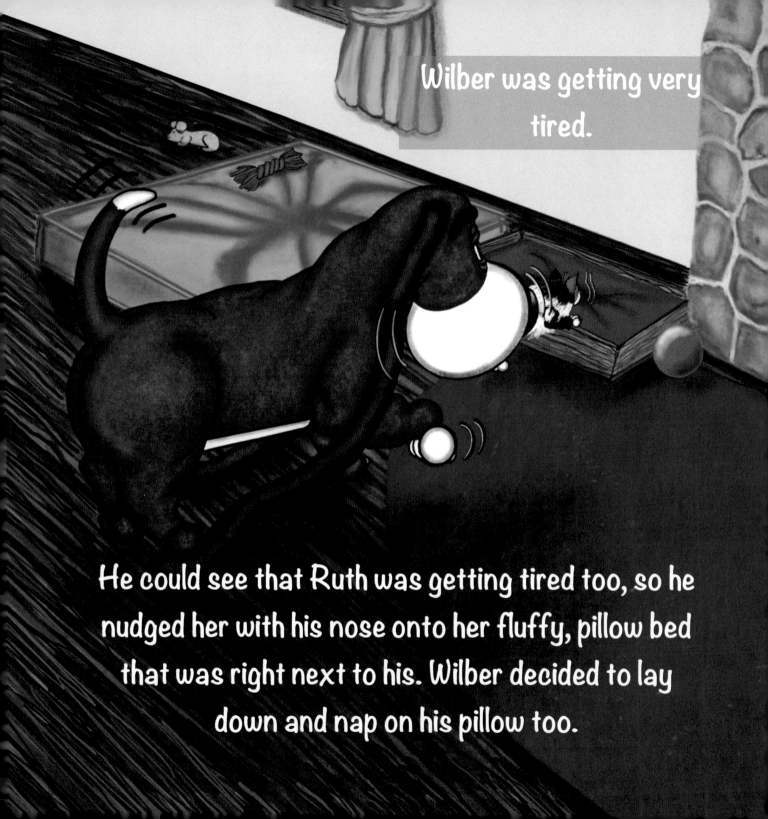

Wilber was getting very tired.

He could see that Ruth was getting tired too, so he nudged her with his nose onto her fluffy, pillow bed that was right next to his. Wilber decided to lay down and nap on his pillow too.

But as soon as Wilber laid down, Ruth came over and climbed on Wilber's pillow, next to him. She pawed at the pillow to make a soft place to lay down, like all kittens do.

Then she cuddled up next to him. Wilber had a
delightfully happy grin on his face as the two fell
fast asleep.

Wilber, Ruth and Oliver became the best friends, ever!

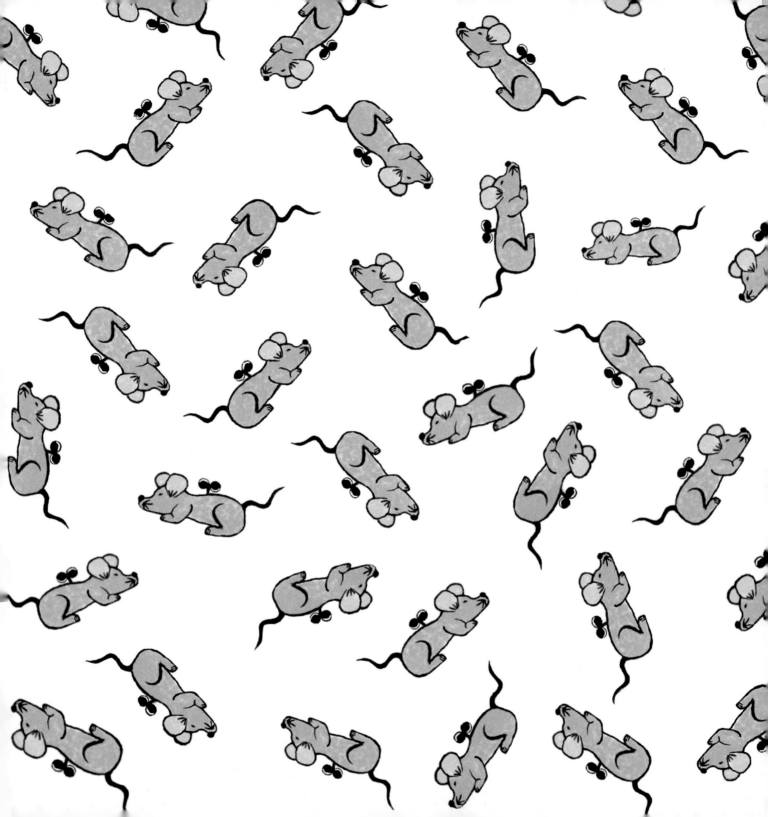

About the Author:

As a young girl growing up in a small town in central Iowa, Collette, a kid at heart herself, is a mother of three grown boys that are now married to their beautiful wives. She now has six young grandchildren, and resides in Clear Lake, Iowa. She is a seasoned multi-media artist, painting on commission and whatever strikes her fancy.

Her character, Wilber, is a drawing from her own creation when her boys were young. Now as an author/illustrator, she is bringing Wilber to life in delightful tales about his adventures.

To all the teachers of our children; be it parents, grandparents, caregivers and educators, the series of Wilber books are created to teach children morals, values, compassion and a little fun, too!

May your home be filled with hugs, love, and caring!

Watch for more Wilber books coming soon.

Made in the USA
Columbia, SC
20 October 2022

69334593R00020